ORANGE JUICE IN DENMARK

WHY AMERICANS ARE SO UNHAPPY

ORANGE JUICE IN DENMARK

WHY AMERICANS ARE SO UNHAPPY

BY
BRADLEY W RASCH

FOREWORD

Orange Juice In Denmark provides an excellent analysis of American depression and unhappiness from a sociological, social psychological, and economic perspective. Rasch, a psychologist, carefully explains why many Americans are unhappy. Do they have too many choices? Are they so overwhelmed with options that there is no satisfying choice to be made?

All readers, regardless of age, will see themselves, and their discontent, within the pages of this book.

Orange Juice in Denmark promises to add a level of insight into the understanding of depression and dissatisfaction not yet seen in the field of psychology.

-Mudcat Herb

INTRODUCTION

Why are people unhappy? This question has been the subject of study in the field of psychology for well over a century. We have learned that in significant cases of unhappiness, depression, there is often a chemical imbalance in the brain itself. We also know that a less potent degree of unhappiness may be due to life events, stressors, or an unwelcoming environment. But what of that feeling of mild dissatisfaction? That general feeling of unhappiness that we cannot link to a life event, or difficult living environment. A general feeling of unhappiness that manifests itself among the wealthy, secure, and well adjusted?

Psychologists have long known that people are uncomfortable when their behavior and belief systems are not well aligned. If we act in a manner that is even slightly discrepant from our beliefs, we feel a degree of discomfort, called cognitive dissonance. To lessen this uncomfortable feeling, we strive to lessen the discrepancy between our actions and our beliefs.

We also feel uncomfortable, and somewhat unhappy, if we feel we have made a wrong decision. We seek to eliminate this unhappiness by confirmation bias. After a decision is made, we tend to not notice things that would suggest that we made the wrong decision, and notice events that confirm the decision that we made. This allows us to be more comfortable and happier.

But what if we cannot ignore things that suggest that we made the wrong decision? If we cannot do this we will have a low-grade sense of unhappiness, of dissatisfaction.

If we have a lingering feeling that we made a wrong decision, on some level, we will be unhappy.

In some cases, we are unhappy, not because we are in a bad situation, but because someone else is in a *better* situation. We compare ourselves to others. Happiness, to a degree, is relative.

The pursuit of happiness is codified in our Declaration of Independence, and is deeply woven into our DNA. When we are happy, chemical neurotransmitters in the brain increase and give us a sense of well-being. We crave this feeling.

According to the World Happiness Report (2012) the United States ranks 23rd in happiness, well behind Iceland, New Zealand, and Denmark, the top three. We are behind our neighbors to the north, the Canadians, even though there are more NHL hockey teams based in the United States.

Is it possible that we sometimes have too many options, too many choices, to be truly happy with our decisions?

This book explores the reasons why Americans are often at least slightly unhappy. It has much to do with orange juice in Denmark and Tim Horton's donuts in Canada. By understanding the causes of this level of dissatisfaction that many of us cope with, we can begin to become happier, and more satisfied with ourselves, our lives, and the people we choose to love and befriend.

We will also explore ways we can become happier within the pages of this book.

CONTENTS

RABBIT EARS
TIN FOIL
AND
THREE CHANNELS

Many readers will have the same memory about television as the author. Those too young to remember the days about to be described have probably heard these stories from their parents, grandparents, aunts or uncles.

There was a time in this country when most homes received only three television stations corresponding to the three major broadcast television networks: ABC, CBS, and NBC. In some cases, if they resided in a populated area, they may also have been able to tune in to an educational channel (what we refer to as PBS today). In even fewer cases, one might have had access to a fifth channel, an independent non-network channel. This was always an independent station, and existed only in major metropolitan areas. These stations, depending on your distance from the city of transmission, provided a picture of varying quality. The quality of reception had much to do with the rabbit ears on top of your television, the amount of tin foil you wrapped around those rabbit ears, or the quality of the antenna you placed on top of your home (only an option for the well-to- do).

When one watched television in these days, at most, they had five options as to what to watch at a given time, and usually no options after 12:30 AM or 1:00 AM as the stations signed off the air at about that time (after the playing of The Star Spangled Banner).

If one was a "late night" television viewer, and wanted to watch a talk show, see all the celebrities, and a first rate monolog, they often had just *one* choice: The Tonight Show, first starring Steve Allen, then Jack Paar, and finally Johnny Carson. When you watched this program, you never had to worry about there being a better guest, or a more entertaining performer on seven or eight other talk shows that may be on at that time. You had only one choice, so you did not even think about the possibility of a "better" talk show to watch. Thus, in many ways, you were quite happy with the show you were seeing. You enjoyed it; you were "in the moment", not needing to worry about something else that might be better or more entertaining. You could apply all your attention (and enjoyment) to the show you were watching.

You had just one choice, and so did everyone else that wanted to stay up late and watch a (the) talk show that night. Because everyone had only one option for scratching his or her talk show itch, everyone had the same experience and could discuss it at work the following morning.

The limited choices people had in these days allowed for not only more satisfaction and enjoyment (people were not worried about missing something that may be better) but for a common experience to discuss with friends and colleagues the following day. This kind of satisfaction and common experience is not really in play today. There are too many options and too few people with common experiences to share the following day.

We are, in some ways, a tad less happy as a result.

THE GINI IN THE BOTTLE

The disciplines of economics, sociology, psychology and political science, along with the United Nations, have agreed on an empirical, scientific method of measuring and describing the levels of equality within a society. This method is called the GINI Index. This statistical methodology allows for the measurement and description of the levels of economic equality within a society, and allows nations to be compared to one another on an "apples to apples" basis. The GINI Index runs from 0 to 100. A 0 represents perfect equality within a society, and a GINI scoring of 100 would represent perfect inequality. In other words, the lower a nations GINI score, the more equal the society is. The GINI Index for the United States is 45.0. Nations with lower scores include Thailand (42.0), The United Kingdom (34.0), Germany (27.0), Iceland (26.0), Denmark (24.0), and Sweden (23.0). It would seem that all of the listed examples (and many nations not listed) are more equal (at least from an economic perspective) than the United States.

We know that people view their happiness, in part, due to how they perceive themselves in relationship to others. We are social creatures; we do evaluate ourselves by our comparisons with other people. We are happy if we are doing well, but we are less happy if we are not doing comparatively well.

By nature, Americans value meritocracy. Those that have greater skills, or skills that are more in demand, are rewarded more. As a society, we are okay with that. We still view ourselves in large part, through the prism of comparison. Many are doing well economically, and it has little to do with their abilities, or societies need for their skills. A lot of folks are doing well because they are members of the "lucky sperm club". They were born into fortunate circumstances. Good circumstances mean access to better schools, an ability to network with other well off people, often with your skill levels being of little relevance. Many of our best schools admit "legacy" students. These students are admitted not due to their credentials, but due to the fact that their parents attended that institution. A degree from this prominent school, often involving many "Gentleman's B's", is the ticket to staying in the upper class.

We are happy to be doing well, but so many people, for reasons that do not seem fair, are often "more equal" than us.

The level of equality, as measured by the GINI Index, often correlates very highly with individuals reported levels of happiness. The more equal a society is, often the happier Its people are.

NOW SHOWING AT A THEATER NEAR YOU

The author hopes that this chapter does not cause you, the reader, to feel as old as the he does. Recently, the author watched the newest James Bond flick at the neighborhood Cinema. At the end of the movie, there was a proud indication that this movie franchise had celebrated its fiftieth year. The Golden anniversary of 007 movies!!

When the first Bond flicks were released, a half century ago, the release was limited. This was true with all films. Only "selected" major cities hosted the film first. It took awhile for the film to make its way to your metropolitan area, even if it was a major metropolitan area. Because the movie had a limited release, and few could go to see it, there was great anticipation that moviegoers had regarding the film. Social Psychology teaches us that when something is scarce, we are more attracted to it.

When the much-anticipated major film made its way to your big city, it was downtown, for quite awhile, before it made its way to suburban theaters. Again, opportunities to see the film were scarce, and movie buffs would leave their suburban homes to see this much talked about movie downtown.

In times past, the "big" movies were savored and enjoyed, because the opportunity to see them was, indeed, scarce. It took a long time for it to arrive at your local theater, and then it was gone. It would not appear on free television for some time. When it did, once again, it was an event.

In current times, movies have a wide release. They appear at thousands of theaters when they open, and sometimes even on demand through your cable television, your computer, or even your cell phone (or a DVD by mail).

These anticipated films are no longer scarce. They can be viewed almost anywhere, and, in many cases, at any time.

Is the ease of seeing a film taking away from our enjoyment of the movie? There is no longer anticipation. We do not have to wait for it, and can see it whenever we want. Social Psychology suggests that this ready supply, and on demand viewing, may well take away some of the satisfaction we derive from watching the movie. We did not have to wait or really jump through any hoops to see it.

Yet another reason why we may enjoy, or appreciate, things a bit less than we used to.

BEER IS PROOF THAT GOD LOVES US AND WANTS US TO BE HAPPY-BEN FRANKLIN

When the author was a teen living in the "Chicagoland Area" a much sought after beer was Coors Beer. Coors Beer was, without a doubt, the Holy Grail of beers, despite Budweiser's claim to be the King of Beers. Why was Coors so popular and sought after?

At the time, Coors was available only west of the Mississippi. So access to it east of the Mississippi, in the Chicago area in particular, was extremely limited. If you wanted to enjoy some Coors, you had to know someone going out west, and beseech them to bring you back a six-pack. If they did, it was like Liquid Gold.

Coors, at the time, was a mythical beer in the Midwest. Everyone's favorite. In large part, because it was so hard to obtain.

Coors was so sought after, that they expanded east of the Mississippi. When that happened, it seemed to loose its cache. It was no longer hard to get, and now one of many beers.

Today, when one goes to an upscale liquor store, now so ubiquitous, that you have several in close proximity to your home, you have a choice of dozens of mass produced beers from around the world, and hundreds of craft beers from just about anywhere. You probably also live within a few miles of several microbreweries.

There are so many beer choices today. Though Ben Franklin would be thankful, perhaps we are not as thankful because we will always have a lingering doubt that we may have left the best beer on the shelf.

So many beers, so little time.

BASEBALL, HOT DOGS, APPLE PIE, AND CHEVROLET

In 1950, Major League Baseball was comprised of sixteen teams placed in just eleven cities (New York had three teams and Boston, St. Louis, Chicago, and Philadelphia had two teams each). Professional baseball in America looked like this:

American League
New York Yankees
Detroit Tigers
Boston Red Sox
Cleveland Indians
Washington Senators
Chicago White Sox
St. Louis Browns
Philadelphia Athletics

National League
Philadelphia Phillies
Brooklyn Dodgers
New York Giants
Boston Braves
St. Louis Cardinals
Cincinnati Reds
Chicago Cubs
Pittsburgh Pirates

Yes, dear readers, the Cubs are actually a major league team.

In 1950 baseball was the national past time. Virtually any male over the age of six could recite the starting lineup of any team. Baseball was a major part of American culture, so much so, that its language found its way into the common language: "Give me a 'ballpark' estimate", "he is out in left field", "I can beat you any day, and twice on Sunday" (this phrase was common in our culture because most teams played two games every Sunday afternoon), "that salesman really struck out when he tried to pitch that product".

In 1950, virtually anyone west of the Mississippi was a Cardinals fan, as there were no teams west of St. Louis. The World Series was a big deal, because only two teams made it to the post season. Fans were very loyal to their teams, in part, because there were so few of them. Because the number of teams was limited to sixteen, most people had a familiarity with every team. Fans were so passionate they listened to games on the radio, and would follow their teams late in the season even when it was certain that they were not going to make it to the World Series.

Contrast baseball of 1950 to baseball of 2014. In 2014, baseball has 30 teams, and 250 more major league ballplayers (if you count the 25 employed by the Cubs). Also, ten teams now qualify for post-season play. When ten teams (instead of two) make the post season, are the regular season games all that important? When there are thirty teams, almost twice as many as existed in 1950, is it that special to have a major league team in *your* city. When there is a limited supply of something, limited choices, (be it the number of teams or teams that qualify for the playoffs) each entity just seems more special and tends to satisfy us a bit more.

In 1950, if you wanted a "nice" luxury car, you had basically two choices a Cadillac (GM) or a Lincoln (Ford). Foreign brands were very rare in this country, and one took a chance owning one in those days because obtaining parts was difficult. When you bought a Lincoln or a Caddie you were generally happy because you did not have to worry about a dozen other cars that might have been better. At this time Lexus, Infiniti, and Acura did not even exist, and Mercedes, BMW, Audi, Jaguars, Porsche, and the others were really not options for most folks because of parts availability, mechanics that could work on them, and so forth.

Today, when one buys that prestige car, after they have owned it for a while, they become cognizant of the fact that there are a dozen other cars that may have been as good or better.

Over a half century ago, you did not have a lot of choices in great hot dogs in your area, or a diner that had a truly great apple pie. When you found it, you *loved* it. You knew it was the best around. Today, you can find upscale hot dogs or pies, boutique stores that feature seven-dollar slices of pie. The author lives near an "encased meat emporium" with truly great hot dogs, excuse me, sausages. In current times, you know there is always a hot dog, a pie, or a car, that will be, or may be, better. Thus, you are not totally satisfied with what you have.

Choice is not a bad thing. It is a good thing. But it seems to have consequences for us. We may not like Root Beer all that much, but if that is the only thing available at a diner during a hot drive thru the desert, it will be the best soda we have ever had.

HAVERNAZATION

When you are about to leave the convenience store after you have made a purchase, the clerk will say, "Have a nice day". Leave the elevator after a conversation with a fellow rider; you will end the ride by hearing or saying, "have a nice day". Get off a plane, get out of a cab, leave the health club, you will be wished a nice day. The average person will hear this 17-20 times a day. We have seen the havernazation of America.

Does this innocuous phrase put pressure on us to have a nice day? What if, for whatever reason, we want to have an adequate day, or even a lousy day?

We also feel required to havernize others, least we offend them. If the President of the United States ended a speech without saying "May God bless you, and may God bless the United States of America" he might be impeached, or at least drop twenty points in each and every opinion poll. Do we feel a similar sanction if we do not havernize people?

This pro forma havernazation may not be so innocuous. It seems to play a small role in promoting our tendency to compare ourselves to others. Are we having as nice a day as they are? Is there a reason they are wishing this, are we having a bad day? Do they think we are having a bad day? Should we be having a bad day?

The increasing havernazation of the American culture involves work, family, and friends. Some evidence suggests that it not only increases our focus on the niceness of our day, but also encourages us to think of other things we might be doing so that we are successfully havernized.

Have a nice day.

SOCIAL MEDIA

Today we can easily be apprised of the lunch preferences, book interests, or skin conditions of people we have not seen in forty years. Often, these are people we did not spend a lot of time with, and did not really notice, forty years ago. We may even have reveled in their skin condition. Today, they are our "friends" and we are aware of every event that occurs in their lives. They post it for us, and all others, to see. Such are the wonders of the Internet and social media.

Psychology has recognized that some folks may just be addicted to the Internet. Its use stimulates the same Neuro chemicals as some street drugs that cause addiction. These chemicals, when released, can give us a sense of pleasure.

When we access social media sites, we quickly compare ourselves to those people, be they significant to us or not. Are we as happy as they are? Have we traveled to places as exotic? Are our children or grandchildren also Dean's List students at an Ivy League University?

Some people without children, that desire to have them, but are unable to, invest time and effort blocking the proud posts and pictures of their friends children.

Never before have we been able to compare our lot in life so readily with vir-tually anyone we have ever known. What may have once been a great day, or great life, may quickly suffer in comparison. What once gave us contentment now tends to give us angst.

We have almost lost our ability to find pleasure in what we have in an age where comparisons are so effortlessly obtainable.

WHITE PAPERS, THE MATING HABITS OF ALBINO TOADS FROM MADAGASCAR, AND WHO REALLY ASSASINATED PRESIDENT KENNEDY

Recently on television (the author receives over 400 channels) during the course of one day there were three separate documentaries being aired on different channels about the Kennedy assassination, five different documentaries about the mating habits of different animals (including albino toads from Madagascar,) I will not allow my miniature Dachshund to watch this channel, and several other documentaries about history ranging from Paul Revere to Richard Nixon (not to be confused with those Albino toads, but perhaps somewhat reptilian nonetheless). It was difficult not to channel surf as there were so many options (I am leaving out some of the compelling ones such as a history of baseball, an expose about faked research on autism, etc). I did do some channel surfing, and was not much enlightened by any of the programs I surfed through. I was constantly wondering: shouldn't I be watching that documentary about_____? There were so many documentaries airing that day, that no one documentary would have been in a position to grab a sizeable audience, there was too much to choose from. If you wanted to discuss any of these documentaries at work the next day with someone, there is a good chance they did not see it, they were watching something else. Those that watched one of the mating documentaries probably would not discuss it at work due to a probable required trip to HR.

Contrast this with what occurred many years ago. Documentaries were rare, of good quality, and viewed by many people. They were always the only documentary on at that time, or even that season. These documentaries were definitely water cooler talk the next day at work. A large enough percentage of viewers watched them, that as a society we had a common experience. They were discussed, were enlightening, and enjoyed. One such documentary, *The Harvest of Shame,* a CBS news "white paper" documentary that brought to light the exploitation of migrant workers, was watched by so many, that it lead to reforms and positive changes. We were moved by this documentary. It impacted us. We watched it, at least in small part, because there were not twelve other documentaries of varying quality we might have watched for fear that it might have been better.

Many such programs and channels are certainly valuable and important, especially in an advanced democratic society. But there is this downside, so often not explored. We often seem less than content with what we are viewing. After all, we have 400 other channels to choose from. Certainly, we feel, there is something better on.

DONUTS IN CANADA

Every year the author and his spouse attend the Stratford Shakespeare Festival in Stratford, Ontario, Canada. Stratford, by American standards, would be a small town in a very rural area, and is not close to a large city. Every summer, since 1953, great plays and musicals with world class actors and directors are performed in this beautiful city. One of the venues is a badminton court during the winter months. Some may be familiar with Stratford being the home of one Justin Beiber.

In recent years, we have taken to staying in a town about eight miles away called St. Mary's. This city is very small. For a late night snack, the only place that is open in St. Mary's is Tim Horton's. Tim Horton's is a donut shop with great coffee. There is limited seating, and depending on the time of day, a limited selection of donuts.

As it is the literally the only place to go certain times of the day, there was a long wait at the drive through (about twenty minutes) and even a lengthy queue to get into the shop to order and eat. People, yours truly and wife included, waited patiently.

Eating at a Tim Horton's is a truly Canadian experience. People are willing to wait, and even clean up after themselves. Tim Horton was a former professional hockey player, giving these shops (Horton's is a chain across all of Canada) a special significance.

Everyone at Tim Horton's truly enjoyed his or her experience.

The donuts we had, the coffee we drank, were the best we had ever tasted. We understood why this place was so beloved by the locals, and so revered in the country. Could the pleasure we took, the donuts we savored so much, have been so good because they were the only game in town? There were not twenty other places to go to *that might have been better.* This was it, and we enjoyed it, as did everyone else.

If you ever up in Canada in a small town, I suggest you visit, preferably late at night when it is the only place open. I guarantee you will love it. So try it, eh?

ORANGE JUICE IN DENMARK

Denmark consistently ranks as one of the happiest countries on the planet. There are a lot of ideas as to why this may be, educated guesses if you will, but no explanation has been scientifically studied. Sociologists, economists, and social psychologists have been interested in the happiness of Danes for quite some time. Possible explanations include health care that won't bankrupt you, a strong social safety net, virtually free higher education, and no wars since World War II.

The author spent a great deal of time in Denmark recently, specifically to explore and inquire about the happy state of the Danes.

While in Copenhagen, the author visited an amusement park, urban refuge, called Tivoli Gardens. Everyone there, mostly local folks, really were enjoying their time there immensely. Their happiness was almost palpable. Everybody, workers and visitors alike, wore broad smiles. With all due respect to Disneyland, this appeared to be the happiest place on earth.

Denmark is a small country. Tivoli Gardens is really the only option in the country for this kind of outing. The people visiting enjoyed being there and took great pride in this place. I should point out, that this beautiful place is dwarfed by several similar places in many Chicago suburbs. In comparison, Tivoli Gardens is smaller with fewer things to do. But Tivoli Gardens is more enjoyed, and appreciated. It is not taken for granted.

I spoke with many Danes about their happiness, and asked why they are often considered the happiest people on our planet. They agreed that they were happy. Their explanations usually involved really appreciating what they had, not what they could have, but what they had. But one wise woman told me things might change. When I asked her why, she said Orange Juice.

She explained that it wasn't that long ago that Orange Juice was not readily available. It was rare and seasonal. And people loved it. Now, she said, it is available everyday. People have it everyday with breakfast, and they do not seem to enjoy it anymore. She feared that their culture would have more Orange Juices, and that the Dane's might loose their happiness.

The next morning, I had tea with breakfast. There was only one kind available. It was really good.

WHAT DOES ALL THIS MEAN?

It is not good to fear change, or to be unhappy with a great deal of choice. Choice is a good thing. Do not be a social Luddite.

When you do make a choice, especially about some thing or activity that may give you pleasure or fulfillment, live that choice. Give it a fair chance. It is not so much the decision you make, but how you live it. Concentrate all your energy on being in the moment. Spend no time worrying about what you could have decided, and very minimal time stressing about a better activity, better thing, or better relationship you might have chosen. You owe it to yourself to give your decision a fair chance. Make this a practice.

By doing so, you are only being fair to others (if it was a relationship decision), or your own level of fulfillment (if it was a job decision), or your contentment (if it was a decision about obtaining a tangible object).

Do not be afraid of changing your mind, but do it when you have truly focused on your initial decision, and giving it, and yourself, a fair chance.

The remaining chapters in this book will address characteristics we can work on, and incorporate into our personality, that will allow us to be a happier and more content person.

VOLUNTEER

One of the best things you can do when you are somewhat unhappy or unfilled, is volunteer. As a general rule, the helper is more helped than the recipient of the goodwill.

We are all social creatures. We are connected to others whether we know them or not. We all need human contact, and have a need to be part of the human community. We feel great when we help others. The chemicals released in our brain that give us a sense of well-being are released through a variety of activities. One of them is helping others.

It is said that no man truly lives until he serves a cause that is bigger than himself. Helping others is such a cause.

Not only does it give us a sense of purpose, and a good feeling to truly help others, we feel as though we are a better person. Our self-esteem is enhanced. When we help others, we do not focus or obsess on what we are unhappy about. We focus on helping.

When we help others, that thank you, that good feeling we instilled in some-one else, is contagious. We catch it.

Many therapists routinely recommend volunteer work for people dealing with minor depression, as a part of their treatment. Returning veterans that are given an opportunity to serve once again, at home, by helping others, often recover much quicker from the psychological effects of war.

By lending a helping hand, you are also helping yourself.

BOOST YOUR CONFIDENCE

Getting to know oneself is an important and worthwhile pursuit. It is essential to be aware of your strengths and weaknesses. When we become keenly aware of our strengths, it not only builds our confidence, but it reminds us that we can use these strengths to compensate for our weaknesses. We may have a specific skill area that is a real weakness for us, accomplishing a task that requires that skill will take us a long time. If we have the strength of a good work ethic, we can get it accomplished.

In some cases in the work place, we may be required to work on a team of people with varying abilities. If we are quick to size up what skills are required, and volunteer to tackle tasks within our area of expertise, where we have strengths, *even if we are doing more than our fair share,* someone else in the group is more likely to address the area involving our weakness.

We can build our confidence by remembering what we have contributed, what we have done well, or will do well, as opposed to focusing only on our weaker area. We all have weak areas, and instead of focusing on them, we need to train ourselves to focus on our attributes that allow us to compensate for them

BE AT PEACE WITH YOURSELF

"God grant us the serenity to accept the things we cannot change, courage to change the things we can, and wisdom to know the difference."
-Dr. Niebuhr

We all have things about ourselves we cannot change. If we are thirty years of age, and four foot ten, we are never going to be tall. By the same token, we all have characteristics that we can change, it may not be pleasant, it may take hard work, but we can change them.

When we take stock of what we are dissatisfied with about ourselves, forget about the things we cannot change, high-light, plan, then change the things we can, we will be happier.

EAT RIGHT AND EXERCISE

Intensive exercise allows us to produce endorphins, a neurotransmitter that produces what is often called a "runners high", or a sense of well-being. Mild depression can often be treated effectively by regular exercise, as opposed to rushing to medication. Not only does exercise actually change our brain's chemistry, it allows us to focus on something other than what is upsetting us. If it is built in as part of our scheduled day, it gives us a positive structure, something we feel good about. Regular intensive exercise can lower our risk for many physical illnesses as well as neurological disorders, including Alzheimer's. In fact, any activity that lessons ones chance for cardiovascular problems also lowers risk for Alzheimer's.

The old computer-programming adage GIGO (Garbage In, Garbage Out) applies to nutrition, mood, and behavior. As our mothers have often told us: "you are what you eat". Eating healthy (especially plenty of fresh fruit and vegetables, and limited sugar and processed food) not only lessens our chances of contracting many diseases (even diseases such as cancer) but also improves the odds that we will not have to deal with depression and a number of other mental health issues.

It pays well to eat well and exercise.

THE IMPORTANCE OF A BUDGET

Financial pressures are stressors for both the single and the married. Very few things can be as stress inducing as financial pressure.

If you are married (and research suggests that people in good marriages are often more happy than single people, or married people in unfulfilling marriages) developing a real budget and sticking to it is important to stress reduction. It removes large bones of contention. This budget, of course, should be mutually constructed.

Money problems are one of those problems that seem to touch every aspect of your life. Avoiding them, having an agreed upon prudent plan, can avoid not only conflict, but also unnecessary stress, stress that will lead to some level of unhappiness.

REMEMBER YOUR FAMILY AND FRIENDS

Most of our happiness in life revolves around our relationship with family and friends. Things are valuable only if they enhance our relationship with family and friends. This is something we all come to realize, often later than we would have wished.

Like anything that we want to last, we need to invest in it. We invest in our home, our education, our careers, and that is all well and good. None of these things, however, are valuable if they do not contribute to our ability to nurture our relationships with family and friends. If you do not invest in something, it will fall apart. All to often, we do not invest in the things that are truly the most important. We need to invest in things relative to their real importance. It is often said that a person facing their last days never regrets not obtaining the extra money they could have made, or the deal they did not make, but regret the time they did not spend with loved ones.

If we invest, as we should, in family and friends, we will be much happier and fulfilled indeed. They will be happier too. It is life's most important win win.

GIVE AND RECEIVE HELP

Giving help to others (nurturance, a strong human need) is a great way to beat the blues. Helping others gives *us* a sense of well-being. We need to give help to be happy and fulfilled. We not only receive psychological benefit by helping others (feeling like a good person, the satisfaction of doing something for someone else, a tenant of all the world's great religions) we feel better as well. Actual chemical changes in the brain give us a sense of pleasure and well-being.

It is also important to accept help when you really need it (succorance). There is a strong human need for succorance.

By seeking help from people that care about us, we lessen our stress, and fulfill the basic human need we all have-succorance.

UNDERSTAND WHAT STESSES YOU AND MANAGE IT

Conduct a little self-examination, and learn what it is that stresses you out. Do this not to focus on the negative, but to make a list of these stressors so that you can develop a plan to minimize or eliminate them, or learn to accept them if they can not be changed. When your list is addressed, resolve to stress about these issues no further. There are now in the past, solved, or accepted.

UNDERSTAND, KNOW, AND EXPRESS YOUR MOODS

One of the valid criticisms of intelligence testing, and theories of intelligence, is that they do not really measure or describe our *emotional intelligence*. Certainly, understanding, recognizing, and using our emotions in a positive or self-serving manner is a sign of intelligence and adaptability. Recognizing our emotions, and expressing them properly, can enhance our lives, reduce stress, and increase contentment.

When Michael Jordon was inducted into the National Basketball Hall of Fame, he thanked the high school coach that cut him from the team. He did this because he *recognized* his emotion of frustration at being cut, and *used* it to motivate himself to excel at the sport he loved.

Holding emotions in is certainly not a way to reduce stress. Expressing them in a hurtful, disrespectful, or combinative manner is also not a positive choice. Recognizing our emotions and expressing them in ways that are socially correct, respectful to others, and us and lead to a solution or improvement is a characteristic of emotional intelligence that can enhance our lives.

SHARE YOUR PROBLEMS WITH SOMEONE IN THE SAME BOAT

We can benefit greatly from sharing our problems with someone that has experienced the same thing. By doing so, we can lend support to them, and also talk with someone that understands exactly what we are going through, that has, in effect, "been there". Returning veterans often can hasten their readjustment by spending time with other veterans, and comparing notes with them. No one else could totally understand what he or she had been, and are going through.

Recovering alcoholics can be key members of support systems for one another. By helping someone else, they can help themselves. They can get support from people that are facing the same challenges.

No one, of course, likes being around a "Debbie Downer". Very few, if any of us, are comfortable spending much time with someone that is whining all the time, a professional victim. But, when someone seeks support from, offers support to, and is motivated to receive and give help, and not to complain for the sake of complaining, sharing problems (and solutions) with someone that has experienced what you have experienced is, more often than not, a very powerful and effective endeavor.

WATCH YOUR URINATION

To paraphrase Frederich Perls (and Marne Gehring) "If you have one foot in the past and one foot in the future, you're pissing on the present".

Life is so much more enjoyable if we *live in the present*. Anytime we obsess on the past, we take energy away from enjoying what is happening now. Whenever we worry obsessively about the future, we have little energy to cope with and enjoy the present.

Being in the moment is a skill worth developing.

2012 HAPPIEST COUNTIRIES ON EARTH

1. Norway
2. Denmark
3. Sweden
4. Australia
5. New Zealand
6. Canada
7. Finland
8. Netherlands
9. Switzerland
10. Ireland

MOST EQUAL COUNTRIES BY GINI INDEX

1. Denmark
2. Japan
3. Sweden
4. Czech Republic
5. Norway
6. Slovakia
7. Bosnia and Herzogavina
8. Hungary
9. Finland
10. Ukraine

MAJOR STRESSORS IN LIFE

1. Relationships- whether it be family relationships, friendships, or significant others. The people you care about most make a huge impact on your life.

2. Money/Finances- Being financially stable can be a huge struggle for many people. And can cause a lot of stress in ones life. Worrying about whether or not you can pay your bills this month can have a negative effect on your health.

3. Employment/Job- This can range from finding a job, job security, poor working environment, or working in a high stress environment.

4. Health- Your personal health, your friends health, your families health or even your pets health. All of these factors can affect your health.

5. Safety- The safety of your friends,family or pets can have a huge impact on the stress in your life. Living in fear can cause a lot of unwanted stress.

6. Home- Your home life can be a stressful environment to live in. Having a huge negative effect on your health.

7. School- A heavy course load, the fear of failure, how are you going to pay your tuition. There could many reasons that school is causing stress in your life.

8. Death- Whether the death causes financial stress, role stress, emotional stress or all of the above. Death is a major life stressor.

9. Retirement- As much as you hear the line "I can't wait to retire". Many people fear whether or not they can afford to retire. Or wonder what they are going to do with their lives after they do retire.

www.ingramcontent.com/pod-product-compliance
Lightning Source LLC
Chambersburg PA
CBHW070812290526
45795CB00002B/691